C·1

SHADOW CATCHER

HOW EDWARD S. CURTIS DOCUMENTED AMERICAN INDIAN DIGNITY AND BEAUTY

by Michael Burgan

Content Adviser: Brett Barker, PhD
Associate Professor of History
University of Wisconsin–Marathon County

COMPASS POINT BOOKS
a capstone imprint

Compass Point Books are published by Capstone,
1710 Roe Crest Drive, North Mankato, Minnesota 56003
www.capstonepub.com

Editor: Catherine Neitge
Designer: Tracy Davies McCabe
Media Researcher: Svetlana Zhurkin
Library Consultant: Kathleen Baxter
Production Specialist: Charmaine Whitman

Image Credits
Charles Deering McCormick Library of Special Collections, Northwestern University
Library, 5, 7, 8, 11, 13, 15, 16, 18, 19, 20, 21, 24, 25, 28, 31, 32, 34, 36, 38, 41,
43, 45, 48, 51 (top), 53, 54, 56 (right), 57 (top, bottom left), 58, 59 (top); Getty
Images: Buyenlarge, 47; Library of Congress, cover, 23, 51 (bottom), 56 (left),
57 (bottom right); Newscom: Cortesia Notimex, 17; Rosemary G. Washington, 59
(bottom); Wikimedia, 27

Library of Congress Cataloging-in-Publication Data
Burgan, Michael.
  Shadow Catcher: how Edward S. Curtis documented American Indian dignity and
beauty / by Michael Burgan.
    pages cm.—(Compass point books. Captured history)
    Includes bibliographical references and index.
    Audience: Ages 10-12.
    Audience: Grades 4-6.
    ISBN 978-0-7565-4992-3 (library binding)
    ISBN 978-0-7565-4998-5 (paperback)
    ISBN 978-0-7565-5008-0 (ebook PDF)
1. Curtis, Edward S., 1868–1952—Juvenile literature. 2. Photographers—United
States—Biography—Juvenile literature. 3. Indians of North America—History—
Juvenile literature. I. Title.
  TR140.C82B87 2015
  973.04'970222—dc23   2014033149

Printed in the United States of America in North Mankato, Minnesota.
092014   008482CGS15

TABLEOFCONTENTS

ChapterOne
THE SHADOW CATCHER

The old man sat staring off into space. He wore a headband, and a blanket surrounded his shoulders. His face was deeply creased from age and decades spent outside in the hot, dry climate of the American Southwest.

In front of the old man, photographer Edward S. Curtis prepared his camera. By now, early in 1905, Curtis was famous across the United States for his photos of the outdoors. His shots ranged from mountain peaks to the huge expanses of the Southwest. People eagerly sat for his portraits, which seemed to capture the essence of the subjects in a single image. Just months before, Curtis had taken pictures of President Theodore Roosevelt and his family. Now Curtis' camera was about to capture the image of Geronimo. The Apache warrior had long been resisting the U.S. government's efforts to keep Indians on reservations. He was the last American Indian to formally surrender to the government.

As a young man, Geronimo had ridden his horse across the vast lands that would become the states of New Mexico and Arizona. He battled Mexicans and then the Americans who tried to end his people's way of life. For 30 years he fought to protect his Apache homeland. His fame grew as he eluded large forces searching for him in craggy mountains and across wide deserts. Finally, in 1886, Geronimo and his Apache followers surrendered.

His shots ranged from mountain peaks to the huge expanse of the Southwest.

"The catching of his features while the old warrior was in a retrospective mood was most fortunate," wrote Edward Curtis in the caption of his 1905 portrait of Geronimo.

With Geronimo's imprisonment, some Americans saw him as part of an era that was fading away. He appeared in Wild West shows that turned some of that history into entertainment. And in 1905 Geronimo was selected to lead the parade at President Roosevelt's inauguration.

That grand event was just a day away when Geronimo sat for Curtis at the Carlisle Indian Industrial School in Carlisle, Pennsylvania. Young Indian children were taken to Carlisle from their reservations to make them more like white Americans and less like Apaches or Crows or whatever their tribe was. But as Curtis' famous picture of Geronimo suggests, even an aged warrior has his pride. The portrait shows a man who is still angry at how his people were treated. He is also a man not ready to give up his people's culture or forget its past. After meeting Geronimo near the end of the warrior's life, Curtis wrote, "The spirit of the Apache is not broken."

By the time he took Geronimo's portrait, Curtis had spent several years living among and photographing many North American tribes. He took formal portraits, just as he had done in his studio in Seattle, Washington. But he also traveled to where the Indians lived and worked. He wanted to document a way of life that he thought might be erased by the spread of white civilization and industrialization. With his photographs, Curtis told a friend, "I want to make them live forever."

In the Territory of Arizona, which was not yet a state, an unknown Indian nicknamed Curtis the "Shadow Catcher" because his photos captured both light and dark so well. Others suggested that the name reflected Curtis' ability to see shadows in a person's heart or soul.

The trips into the Southwest were needed to achieve Curtis' great goal—to record the lives of Indians from

After meeting Geronimo near the end of the warrior's life, Curtis wrote, "The spirit of the Apache is not broken."

Curtis' camera captured, as he wrote in 1907, "a scene in the high mountains of Apache-land just before the breaking rainstorm."

the Great Plains to the Pacific, as far north as Alaska. But Curtis wanted to do more than use his considerable photographic skills. He planned to learn about the tribes' religions and daily lives, hear their myths, and write down their languages. Using a wax cylinder, he would record the sounds of the Indians' words and music. And he used an early movie camera to document even more of American Indian life. No one had ever tried to do what Curtis hoped to do—to study so many tribes in such detail.

Curtis wanted to share what he learned in a large set of books he called *The North American Indian*. He felt great urgency to complete this monumental mission before the traditional ways of Indian culture disappeared forever. When Curtis described his idea to Theodore Roosevelt,

In the Bad Lands appeared in Volume 3 of Edward Curtis' 20-volume work.

the president replied, "No man could be doing anything more important."

Curtis' great project would have been bold for anyone to try, but perhaps even more so for someone with his background. Most scholars who studied the country's Indian tribes had completed years of formal preparation. Curtis' education ended after elementary school in Minnesota, where he spent most of his childhood.

But Curtis received a different kind of education while traveling through the state's backcountry. During the 1870s his father, Johnson Curtis, was a preacher who traveled by canoe to visit members of his church. He took young Edward with him, and the boy learned how to hunt, camp, and survive in harsh conditions.

Curtis also gave his son something else—a camera lens he had brought home from the Civil War. Following instructions in a photography magazine, Edward built his own simple camera. For most of his life, he would combine his love of the outdoors with his interest in taking pictures.

In 1887 the Curtis family headed west and settled near Seattle. Curtis took a variety of jobs, but photography seemed to have stuck in his mind. Some time around 1890, he bought a camera. His wooden box camera was completely unlike today's digital cameras. Big and bulky and weighing more than 20 pounds (9 kilograms), the camera had to sit on a tripod to keep it steady. Curtis would drape a black cloth over his head when taking a picture, to keep unwanted light from affecting the negative. The camera recorded images on a 14x17-inch (36x43-centimeter) glass plate. Though large and fragile, the glass plates could be used to create photos with great detail. Each photo required a new glass-plate negative. After the images were on the plates, Curtis made prints, creating photos others could see—and buy.

That was Curtis' plan—to use the camera to take pictures of people at a studio in Seattle. The people would pay him for their portraits. First, though, he had to learn something about studio photography. He bought a share of an established studio, and his new partner taught him the craft. Soon he moved to another studio and acquired more skills, while also studying the work of great photographers of the day. Along the way, he had met and married Clara Phillips and started a family.

In just a few years, Curtis became one of Seattle's leading photographers. He had a gift for composition— arranging the placement of objects in his pictures. Along with taking studio portraits, Curtis also ventured outside with his camera, though he often used one much smaller than his first big wooden camera. In 1895 he began to photograph some of the Indians who remained in Seattle even as more white settlers flooded in.

The most famous Indian in Seattle then was a woman the white residents called Princess Angeline. She was the elderly daughter of Sealth, a Suquamish chief in the region. Sealth was also known as Chief Seattle, and the city was named for him. One day Curtis saw Angeline

Princess Angeline, the daughter of Chief Seattle, posed for a formal portrait. Angeline at work was the subject of *Clam Digger*. Both images appeared in Volume 9 of *The North American Indian*.

near the shore, gathering clams and mussels. As he later recalled, "The first photograph I ever made of Indians was of Princess Angeline." Curtis took several photos of her working and a formal portrait, which later appeared in *The North American Indian*.

In 1898 Curtis entered two of his pictures of Angeline in a National Photographic Society exhibition. A third, called *Homeward*, showed several Puget Sound Indians paddling a canoe. It won the exhibition's top prize and boosted Curtis' fame.

Just outside Seattle stands 14,410-foot-high (4,392-meter-high) Mount Rainier. Curtis loved to explore it and other peaks in the region, lugging his photography equipment with him. On one trip he made a daring rescue of another climber who had slipped and fallen into some rocks. On another trip in 1898, he encountered a group of climbers ready to walk onto a huge glacier as night fell. For their safety, Curtis invited them to spend the night at his camp instead. The climbers agreed, and Curtis soon found himself talking with several famous men.

One was Gifford Pinchot, who would become the first director of the U.S. Forest Service. Another was George Bird Grinnell, founder of the Audubon Society. The group worked to protect birds and their habitat. Through the men he met on Mount Rainier, Curtis was invited the next year to serve as a photographer with a scientific expedition to Alaska. He took several thousand pictures, including many of the native people there. Although Curtis, like others of the time, incorrectly called all the people "Eskimos," the tribes had distinct cultures.

The Alaska trip gave Curtis a chance to become good friends with Grinnell, who was an expert on American Indians of the Great Plains. He influenced Curtis' later view that the Indian way of life was dying. Grinnell invited Curtis on a trip that would change his life.

Through the men he met on Mount Rainier, Curtis was invited the next year to serve as a photographer with a scientific expedition to Alaska.

ART AND CRAFT

Homeward *appeared in Volume 9 of* The North American Indian.

Homeward and many other Curtis photographs showed the influence of an early style of photography often called pictorialism. Photographers tried to create images that suggested fine-art paintings, rather than merely recording the subjects.

Curtis and other photographers paid careful attention to shadows and the backgrounds in their shots. Special lenses could create a soft focus that resulted in an almost dreamy image. Describing Curtis' first Indian photos, biographer Anne Makepeace wrote, "He used light and composition to create the illusion of a timeless presence untouched by change." Along with studying the art of taking beautiful pictures, Curtis also mastered the use of chemicals and processes when making prints. He worked with photogravure, a process that involved etching the image onto a copper plate. The plate was used to make final prints with remarkable detail.

Curtis also developed prints he called Curt-tones; they are often called goldtones or orotones. A gold-colored metal powder used during the developing process gave the entire picture a golden glow.

ChapterTwo
QUEST FOR PHOTOS—AND MONEY

A trip in 1900 took Edward Curtis to Montana with George Bird Grinnell to see a great Indian religious ceremony, the Sun Dance. He was amazed at what he saw. Stretched out before him was a field of tepees, perhaps 200. They belonged to various branches of the Blackfeet Nation. The Indians gathered to build a lodge. Then, over several days, they danced and chanted, trying to strengthen their relationship with the land and all living beings. Grinnell thought this might be Curtis' only chance to see a Sun Dance. The U.S. government had outlawed it and other forms of traditional Indian religious life as part of its effort to make the Indians more like white Americans.

Along with his camera equipment Curtis brought a wax cylinder recorder. The machine was one of the first made to record sound. The sound vibrations made a metal needle go up and down as it traveled over the wax. The needle on a cylinder player played back the sounds. The wax cylinders could be easily damaged by dirt or heat, but Curtis was determined to record the Indians' words and music.

Grinnell took Curtis down to the Blackfeet camp, so he could get to know them as people, not just subjects for his camera and recorder. Some of the Indians were suspicious of Curtis and his strange equipment. One, named Small Leggins, charged at Curtis on horseback. A chief who liked Curtis saved his life. Curtis later said that he became

Young Piegan horsemen rode toward the Sun Dance encampment with willows for a sweat lodge. The image appeared in Volume 6 of Curtis' work.

friendly with Small Leggins, "but he never lost his distrust for the camera."

While Curtis photographed the Piegan, the main band of the Blackfeet taking part in the Sun Dance, he also listened to their words, their myths, and their history. It was in 1900 that he came up with the idea that would lead to *The North American Indian*. He had earlier written to Grinnell that "the Indians of North America are vanishing. There won't be anything left of them in a few generations and it's a tragedy—a national tragedy. ... I believe I can do something about it. ... I'm a poor man but I've got my health, plenty of steam and something to work for."

The idea of the "vanishing Indian" was common among some white Americans of the day. They focused on the movement of settlers west and how they set up new communities—often on land the Indians used for hunting. The whites chose to ignore the Indians who were still there—the Indians trying to live their lives as they always had. But the notion of the vanishing Indians struck a chord with Curtis and others. It was easier, in a way, to think of them as being part of the past, rather than try

Curtis described his image of "three proud old leaders" in Volume 6 as "a glimpse of the life and conditions which are on the verge of extinction."

A self-portrait of Edward Curtis in about 1889.

to improve their lives or treat them fairly in the present. Curtis, though, had more respect for American Indians and their culture than many other people did.

Curtis was soon on the road again with his equipment, this time to Hopi lands in Arizona. The Hopi let him document part of their most important ritual, the Snake

In the caption for the formal portrait of his friend Honovi, Curtis explained what the Hopi snake dancer was holding: "The right hand grasps a pair of eagle feathers—the 'snake whip'—and the left a bag of ceremonial meal." The image appeared in Volume 12.

Dance, which was a prayer for water. Specially trained priests collected rattlesnakes and then brought them back to villages for the ceremony. The priests danced and talked to the snakes, asking for rain. Released back to the wild, the snakes were supposed to take this message to the gods. Curtis was fascinated with the Snake Dance and asked to take part. It took several years of visiting the Hopi before he got his wish, learning the secrets of the ritual.

Curtis titled his photo of young Hopi women, which appeared in Volume 12, *East Mesa Girls.*

Leaving the Hopi after his first visit, Curtis went back to Seattle and his studio business, but each summer he went back into the field to do research. He spent time in the Pacific Northwest and the Southwest. The tribes he visited included the Navajo, the Havasupai, and the Pueblo. While he was gone, Clara Curtis ran his studio, with other photographers doing the work. Curtis hoped the money his studio made taking pictures of wealthy Seattle residents would pay his bills. By 1901 he was

decorating the studio with Indian art, highlighting for customers his work with the tribes.

In the fall of 1903, instead of Curtis' seeking out an Indian subject, one came to him. The Washington Historical Society had invited Chief Joseph of the Nez Perce to the city. Like Geronimo of the Apache, Joseph had tried to help his people avoid being forced to live on a reservation. In 1877 the Nez Perce battled U.S. troops as they tried to keep their lands in the Pacific Northwest. Joseph was not a great warrior; he saw himself more as a diplomat, trying to help his people

Curtis explained to his readers that the four-armed crosses in Pima baskets could represent the four directions of the wind.

Curtis wrote in Volume 8 that "The name Chief Joseph is better known than that of any other Northwestern Indian."

avoid complete destruction. When Curtis met him, the Nez Perce statesman was near the end of his life. He sat for several pictures, including one that became another of Curtis' most famous Indian portraits. The picture, Curtis biographer Timothy Egan wrote, shows "Joseph's extraordinary face: scars and nicks, prominent lines formed from habitual sorrow."

Curtis went to Washington, D.C., in 1903, hoping to get money from the Smithsonian Institution for his work. Three years into his project, Curtis had not reduced the scope of it. In fact, he wanted to do more—soon he would be filming the tribes. He also needed to hire people to help him do his fieldwork and he needed to pay his staff in Seattle. The Smithsonian had ethnologists and others doing research about Indian tribes. Perhaps it would have some money for Curtis.

The photographer, however, was disappointed with the response he got. The experts at the Smithsonian thought his plan to record the lives of 80 tribes was impossible. Perhaps some of them wondered whether Curtis, with just his elementary school education, had the necessary skills. Curtis wrote afterward, "They say I am trying to do the work of fifty men and don't believe I can do it!" Curtis also failed to garner financial support when he went to see a New York publisher, who had no interest in a book about American Indians.

Soon, however, Curtis thought his luck might have turned for the better. A national magazine sponsored a contest to find "the prettiest child in America." The winning photos of several children would be used as sources for oil paintings. Clara Curtis entered one of her husband's pictures of a local girl. The photo was chosen as a winner, and the painter told President Theodore Roosevelt about the quality of Curtis' work. The president was looking for someone to photograph him and his energetic family. He chose Curtis.

The experts at the Smithsonian thought his plan to record the lives of 80 tribes was impossible.

Curtis photographed young Quentin Roosevelt catching june bugs in a field of daisies at Sagamore Hill, President Theodore Roosevelt's Long Island home.

So in June 1904, instead of photographing Indians, Curtis headed to the president's home at Oyster Bay, Long Island. He spent his days playing with the Roosevelt children and talking with the president. Curtis explained his project, and Roosevelt was intrigued. He loved history, and he had spent time, as he put it, in "the Wild West ... the West of the Indian and the buffalo-hunter, the soldier and the cow-puncher." Roosevelt had invested in two cattle ranches years before in what would become North

Dakota, and on many hunting expeditions he had camped under the stars, as Curtis did.

Curtis showed Roosevelt his recent portrait of Chief Joseph, as well as pictures of the Hopi and Navajo.

PRESIDENT ROOSEVELT'S VIEWS

Curtis photographed masked Apache men demonstrating the Dance of the Gods for Volume 1.

In his younger years, like many people of his day, Theodore Roosevelt did not think highly of most American Indians. Among the many books he wrote was a four-volume history called *The Winning of the West*, which was published from 1889 to 1896. In it, Roosevelt wrote that it was "warped" to think that white Europeans should not have taken the western lands where the Indians lived. He called them "a few scattered savage tribes." And the white settlers who drove them from their lands, he wrote, had done the country a great service. Once the Indians were defeated, Roosevelt hoped, they would adopt what he thought was the superior white American way of life.

He softened his views on Indians as individuals after serving with some during the Spanish-American War. Fighting in Cuba, he led a group of soldiers known as Rough Riders. Several were American Indians from the West. He praised them for their skill and dedication to the country. Yet in the same writing, he referred to the Apaches his soldiers had previously fought against in the Southwest as "the most bloodthirsty and the wildest of all the red men." Still, when Edward Curtis described his great project, Roosevelt was open to it. The president, like others, accepted the idea of the vanishing Indians. Some of his friends who had studied Indian culture had convinced him of the value of documenting it.

Roosevelt saw the obvious quality of Curtis' work, and he believed the project was worthwhile. The president didn't offer any money or specific aid, at least not then. But when the first volume of *The North American Indian* was published in 1907, Roosevelt provided the foreword that opened the book. He wrote, "In Mr. Curtis we have both an artist and a trained observer, whose pictures are pictures, not merely photographs; whose work has far more than mere accuracy, because it is truthful."

Before Curtis left the Roosevelts, he persuaded the president to sit for a portrait. The image is one of the best known of "TR," and the print features Curtis' orotone process. Roosevelt wore his usual pince-nez glasses and a serious look. Curtis wrote excitedly about the picture to Gifford Pinchot, who worked for the president. "My picture of the President is great. It is quite different from anything before taken and, I believe, will be considered by all who know him, a splendid likeness." Curtis explained that he placed most of the portrait in shadow, "bringing the face, with its great strength of character, the only thing that we see, and I believe it is good." Jacob Riis, a well-known journalist, photographer, and social reformer of the era, agreed. "The picture of the President," he wrote, "I will always maintain, is more than a picture, it is the man himself. I did not know that it was possible for photographs to do just that."

Having President Roosevelt's backing boosted Curtis' spirits. But he still had to do the hard work out in the field

> "The picture of the President, I will always maintain, is more than a picture, it is the man himself. I did not know that it was possible for photographs to do just that."

and pay his helpers. He still needed money—lots of it. In January 1906 he approached one of the richest men in the world, J. P. Morgan. His company had put up money to build the Brooklyn Bridge and would later finance the Panama Canal. Just five years before Curtis' visit, Morgan

had created the world's largest company, U.S. Steel. His money had also helped pay for the railroads that took white settlers west—and played a part in disrupting Indian life on the Plains. Morgan was not known as a student of Indian culture, but he did appreciate fine art. He could see the skill and artistry in the photos Curtis showed him.

One of these was *At the Old Well of Acoma*, taken in the Acoma Pueblo in New Mexico. Another was a portrait of a Mojave Indian girl named Mosa.

Curtis told Morgan he had already spent his life savings on the project but was not close to finishing. He asked the banker to give him $15,000 a year for five years. Curtis also asked for money to publish his planned 20-volume book set. Merely publishing his work was not enough. Curtis wanted the books to have the finest paper and binding possible. And he would use photogravure to make the pictures sparkle with detail.

Morgan listened to Curtis, and then agreed—to a point. He would provide money for fieldwork, but not for printing. Curtis would have to earn that by persuading purchasers, including libraries and museums, to buy *The North American Indian* even before it was finished. Morgan also convinced Curtis to write the text for the books himself. Curtis agreed, though others eventually helped him with that part of the project. Curtis was thrilled to have Morgan's support. As he prepared to leave, Morgan told him, "I like a man who attempts the impossible."

But even with Morgan's money, Curtis might have felt at times that the impossible was still ahead.

"I like a man who attempts the impossible."

ChapterThree
SUCCESSES AND STRUGGLES

With funding secure for at least part of his project, Edward Curtis returned to the field. He spent time in 1906 with the Apache in eastern Arizona. Traveling with him and his team of assistants was his 12-year-old son, Hal. By now, Curtis had another nickname that his crew had given him—the Chief.

Curtis had been with the Apache the year before and had taken many photos, but the Indians had refused to discuss their religion. Supposed experts at the Smithsonian had even told Curtis the tribe had no religion. But this time, flush with cash, Curtis was able to buy access to the Apache's religious secrets. He photographed a sacred document that explained the Apache creation myth. Then he persuaded a shaman, Goshonne, to explain the document's meaning. His friendship with Goshonne also helped Curtis get portraits of several Apaches.

The next year Curtis released the first volume of *The North American Indian*, which consisted of a bound book and an accompanying portfolio with loose sheets. Volume I focused on the Navajo and the Apache and opened with a note from President Roosevelt praising the project. The first portfolio sheet displayed a photo Curtis called *The Vanishing Race*. The title reflected Curtis' belief that the Indian way of life was dying, and the photo suggests the theme. A line of Navajo on horseback ride

Portfolio 1, plate no. 1, *The Vanishing Race*. In his caption, Curtis wrote: "Feeling that the picture expresses so much of the thought that inspired the entire work, the author has chosen it as the first of the series."

away from the camera and into shadows—as Curtis wrote, "into the darkness of an unknown future." One rider looks back at the camera, as if looking back at the way of life the Indians are leaving behind. Curtis and his assistant Adolph Muhr had spent hours processing the negative to get the exact print Curtis wanted. *The Vanishing Race* would become one of Curtis' most famous photos, as much for the theme as the image.

Perhaps the most striking picture in the portfolio

Curtis descibed Arizona's Cañon de Chelly (pronounced *de shay*) as a "wonderfully scenic spot" in the heart of Navajo country.

is of Cañon de Chelly. The stark, high walls of the rock canyon serve as a backdrop for a group of Navajo riding by. Nature, in the form of the canyon, dwarfs the humans, and reminds the viewers of the permanence of the rocks compared with the short span of a person's life. And yet the Navajo comfortably live in what others might see as a harsh, unwelcoming environment.

Curtis wrote in the first volume that he had come to know how important all facets of nature were to the Indians. Their story, he said, "is a record of the Indian's relations with and his dependence on the phenomena of the universe—the trees and shrubs, the sun and stars, the lightning and rain." Curtis, of course, also immersed himself in nature to get his photos and do his research. He described for his readers where he was when he wrote what they were reading: by a brook in a forest, near a tree that a beaver had just cut down, while birds sang overhead.

Curtis also explained that, while he was primarily a photographer, "I do not see or think photographically." Perhaps he was referring to the influence of pictorialism on his work. He said he would avoid microscopic detail to present the Indians' stories "as a broad and luminous picture."

In the text Curtis described things that he couldn't capture with his camera, such as the way the Apache loved to swap jokes and play pranks. And while he sometimes used the words *savage* and *primitive*, Curtis wanted

Curtis described Apache women's clothing in his caption for *Jicarilla Maiden* in Volume 1: beaded deerskin cape, deerskin dress, black leather belt, and hair fastened with a large knot of yarn or cloth.

people to know that Indians were humans, just as his readers were, even if their lives were very different. The Indians, he thought, did not want the "civilization" of the white Americans. They wanted to live as they always had, practicing their religions as they always had. But the laws and requirements of the U.S. government prevented that. Curtis' belief that government officials and Christian missionaries made life worse for the Indians only strengthened over time.

The first volume of *The North American Indian* awed the critics who read it. Reviewing the first two volumes in 1908, a *New York Times* critic said Curtis had done something that had never been done before and would never be done again. The reviewer particularly praised his photographic skills: "Mr. Curtis has rare qualities as a photographer, alike in his recognition of the groupings, the light and shade, the points of view that will make a picture as pleasing as it is truthful, and in his ability to make the picture after he recognizes its value." A *Unity Magazine* reviewer in Chicago called the work "the most wonderful publishing enterprise ever undertaken in America." Some ethnologists also saw the value of Curtis' work. They praised him for his contribution to scholars' knowledge of Indian culture. Visiting President Roosevelt in Washington D.C., Curtis was treated like a hero.

But even with the glowing reviews, Curtis failed to sell all 500 sets of *The North American Indian* that he had planned to publish. Its cost—originally $3,000 for the 20-volume set, then rising over time to $4,200—even scared away many of the wealthiest potential customers. Curtis sank into debt from the publishing expenses, even as J. P. Morgan's money helped with the research.

During the summer of 1907, Curtis traveled first to Montana, then to South Dakota, which he had visited two years before. By now he had the help of Alexander

A portrait of Alexander Upshaw, Curtis' friend and translator, appeared in Volume 4.

Upshaw to pave the way with the various tribes and serve as translator. A Crow, Upshaw had been educated at the Carlisle Indian Industrial School in Pennsylvania and then had studied religion before returning to his home in Montana. Although educated by and comfortable with whites, Upshaw wanted to defend the traditional rights of

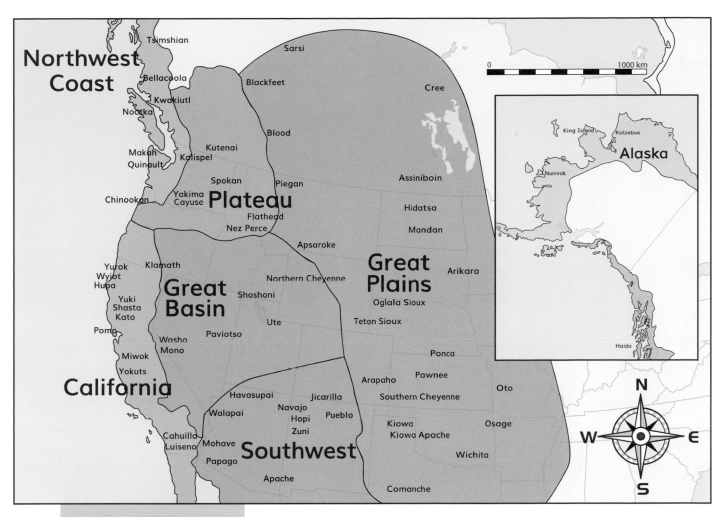

Northwest Coast

Tsimshian
Bellacoola
Kwakiutl
Nootka
Makah
Quinault
Chinookan

Sarsi
Blackfeet
Cree
Blood
Kutenai
Kalispel
Spokan
Piegan
Assiniboin

Plateau
Yakima
Cayuse
Flathead
Nez Perce

Hidatsa
Mandan

Apsaroke

Yurok
Wyiot
Hupa
Yuki
Shasta
Kato
Pomo
Miwok
Yokuts

Klamath

Great
Basin

Shoshoni

Ute

Washo
Mono

Paviotso

Northern Cheyenne

Great
Plains

Arikara

Oglala Sioux

Teton Sioux

Ponca

California

Havasupai
Walapai
Navajo
Hopi
Zuni
Cahuilla
Luiseno
Mohave
Papago
Apache

Jicarilla

Pueblo

Southwest

Arapaho
Southern Cheyenne

Pawnee

Oto

Kiowa
Kiowa Apache

Osage

Wichita

Comanche

0   1000 km

Alaska
King Island   Kotzebue
Nunivak

Haida

N
W   E
S

Curtis studied and photographed Indian tribes from the Great Plains to Alaska.

the tribes. His views may have helped Curtis understand how whites had, as Upshaw once said, "robbed us of our land, our strength, our dignity, our content."

In South Dakota Curtis visited Lakota Sioux lands and met with Chief Red Hawk. He and Curtis had become friends on the photographer's previous trip to the region. Red Hawk had posed in 1905 for a picture that would become another of Curtis' most famous, *An Oasis in the Bad Lands*. On the 1905 trip, Curtis had promised to return and hold a feast for Red Hawk and 20 of his

Curtis' 1905 picture of Red Hawk, *An Oasis in the Bad Lands,* appeared in Volume 3.

men—a way to earn their cooperation for the photos he wanted of them. Instead Curtis found several hundred Lakota waiting for the planned feast! Curtis sent his son, Hal, to get more beef, and the festivities went on.

Curtis had the Lakota reenact actions from their past. They wore headdresses made with feathers they would have earned performing courageous acts in battle. Curtis gave the pictures such titles as *The Morning Attack* and *Brule war-party*. There was no attack, of course, and no war. The various branches of the Lakota, like the other tribes Curtis met, lived on reservations and no longer battled anyone. But the images, with Curtis' captions, captured what had been real just several decades before.

Edmond Meany, a scholar of American Indians and a friend of Curtis', was on the 1907 expedition. He marveled at how Curtis got closer to the Indians than any of the so-called experts. Meany reported that one Lakota chief said, "How did you learn to be just like the Indians?" Of course the photographer was not just like the Indians, but he attempted to understand them and their culture as few whites had.

On the 1907 trip, Curtis also met several of the Crow scouts who had ridden with Lieutenant Colonel George Custer at the Battle of the Little Bighorn. In that 1876 clash in eastern Montana, Sitting Bull and other Lakota chiefs fought to hold on to their traditional lands. They overwhelmed Custer's forces and scored a decisive victory.

With the scouts leading the way, Curtis walked over

the battlefield where white Americans and Lakota had fought. From what he heard from the scouts and saw for himself, Curtis became convinced that the accepted belief was wrong. Custer had not been a tragic hero. Unlike most Americans of the time, Curtis was willing to ignore popular opinion and see history from the Indians' perspective.

Before Curtis, few people had challenged the accepted white view of the history of the Little Bighorn battle. Scholars did not seek out the views of Indians to get their side of the story, whether they fought for Custer or against him. Curtis saw that the Indians' version of the facts, based on their own experience, could be just as true, if not more so, than the words of white soldiers and government officials. Seeing the importance of the Indians' view of history reflected Curtis' larger respect for Indian culture and rituals. He saw their value as people, rather than viewing them as "savages," as some white Americans did. Still, Curtis believed that Indians would be better off accepting the lifestyle of white Americans, since progress had disrupted their old ways. His attitude could be called paternalistic—he thought the Indians needed the white man's help to survive. But for his day, Curtis was quite enlightened.

After the release of the first volume of *The North American Indian*, more volumes followed fairly quickly. Eight had been published by 1911. The Indians featured included the Nez Perce and neighboring tribes; Plains

Seeing the importance of the Indians' view of history reflected Curtis' larger respect for Indian culture and rituals.

Indians, such as the Crow and Blackfeet; and tribes that lived between the Rockies and Cascade Mountains, such as the Kutenai. One of Curtis' more artful works shows a Kutenai in a canoe gathering rushes on a lake. The rushes frame and partly hide the canoe, which is a dark shape against the lighter-toned water, mountains, and sky. The thin, crisp rushes, standing straight up, also provide a contrast to the many horizontal elements of the picture.

Curtis also kept busy raising money—there never seemed to be enough—and continuing his work in the field. His crew set out for British Columbia, Canada, in 1910 and worked with the Kwakiutl of Vancouver Island. As in the United States, Curtis got to photograph ceremonies that the government had banned. Over the next several years, the Curtis team returned several times to record Kwakiutl life, and Curtis shot a movie there, *In The Land of the Head Hunters*. As filmmakers might do in Hollywood, Curtis hired men to build sets that looked like Kwakiutl villages of old.

By the time Curtis released the film, World War I had started in Europe. The war made it hard to sell subscriptions to *The North American Indian* and to buy the fine paper Curtis used to print the books. With money short, his crew shrank in number and sometimes went without pay. Volume 10, focusing on the Kwakiutl, came out during the war, in 1915. Volume 11, featuring the Nootka and the Haida, followed in 1916. But the next volume would not appear until 1922, featuring one of the first tribes Curtis had studied, the Hopi. His images showed readers the distinct round buns of hair Hopi girls wore and the snake priests performing some of the public parts of the Snake Dance.

By now Curtis had new challenges. His wife, Clara, had divorced him and won control of his Seattle studio. He moved to Los Angeles and opened a new studio. He also made money working for movie companies, running movie cameras and taking pictures of the actors. But finishing all 20 volumes of *The North American Indian* was still his major goal.

CURTIS AND HIS FILM

Curtis' 1914 photo of a Kwakiutl wedding party was taken during movie filming. It appeared in Volume 10.

Not content to make a real documentary, Edward Curtis turned *In the Land of the Head Hunters* into a sort of love story. Two characters fall in love, then the woman is captured by an evil sorcerer, sparking a war. Along the way Curtis added things that were not part of Kwakiutl life. But to film critics, the movie brilliantly showed a side of Indian life that few whites had seen. Curtis showed his work to another filmmaker, Robert Flaherty, in 1915. Several years later Flaherty released *Nanook of the North*, a film about Inuit life. Flaherty was greatly influenced by Curtis' work, and Nanook became one of the most famous documentaries of all time.

In the Land of the Head Hunters, however, wasn't widely distributed during Curtis' lifetime. In 1924 Curtis sold his rights to it for $1,000, after spending $75,000 to make it. The showing of a restored version of the movie, accompanied by a live orchestra, headlined the Seattle International Film Festival in 2008.

ChapterFour
"THE CAUSE" LIVES ON

During his many years of work on *The North American Indian*, Edward Curtis started calling his huge project "the Cause." Learning all he could about the Indians and sharing that knowledge with the world defined the meaning of his life. So even as he struggled to support himself with his film work and money he received from his daughter Beth, he thought about completing his fieldwork. In 1922 he photographed tribes in northern California. The next volumes of the set appeared two years later, and that same year, Curtis helped start the Indian Welfare League. The group fought to make Indians U.S. citizens and give them the right to vote. Through the work of the league and other groups, all American Indians became U.S. citizens in 1924.

Curtis returned to Alaska in 1927, this time visiting islands he had not gone to on the 1899 expedition. Curtis bought a boat in Nome, Alaska. With his daughter Beth and an assistant, he sailed to Nunivak and other islands in the Bering Sea. The trip had its dangers, as a storm sent waves much higher than the boat crashing down on it. But Curtis was thrilled to be learning about Indians who had little knowledge of western culture. "At last," he wrote, "... I have found a place where no missionary has worked." He wrote that the people of Nunivak were the happiest people he had met on his travels. He thought lack

of contact with whites explained their happiness.

By this time, Volume 17 had been published, and the rest would come over the next three years. The pictures from this Alaskan trip appeared in the last volume of *The North American Indian*, which came out in 1930. Unlike the first two volumes, which had received such praise, the last one was barely noticed in the newspapers or by scholars. Curtis, who had once toured the country showing his work, was now largely forgotten. The lack of response disapppointed him.

Since 1928 Curtis had not even owned all the work he had done over three decades. Now it all belonged to the Morgan Company, run by J. P. Morgan's son. The Morgan family had given Curtis $400,000 over the years, yet he was broke and would never make money from "the Cause." He later wrote, "When I was through with the last volume, I did not possess enough money to buy a ham sandwich."

Curtis put aside photography for a time and began hunting for gold in the mountains of California. The country was in the middle of the Great Depression, when millions of people had lost their jobs and their homes. Beth continued to support her father, who for a time returned to Hollywood to take pictures on a movie set and on location in Montana and the Dakotas. The tough times meant Curtis had trouble selling the remaining complete sets of *The North American Indian*. Even the Morgan Company lost interest in Curtis' work. In 1935 it sold the prints and negatives it owned to Charles E. Lauriat Jr., a Boston rare-book dealer. Lauriat paid just $1,000 for this unique piece of American history.

Curtis, once an adventurer who climbed mountains, crossed deserts, and braved rattlesnakes, spent some of his last years living on a California farm or in a small Los Angeles apartment. His great work was largely forgotten, though he believed it would remain "the outstanding story of the Indians." When he died in 1952,

Curtis (in white shirt next to tent) spent months living among the people he photographed.

at age 84, *The New York Times* ran just a short article. The paper called him an "internationally known authority on the history of the North American Indian." Without giving the name of the 20-volume work, the obituary referred to the "monumental" set of books Curtis had produced. It closed by noting that he "was also widely known as a photographer." In 1952, though, that fame as a photographer was largely in the past. And the negatives, prints, and photogravures that Charles Lauriat had bought 17 years before sat gathering dust in a Boston basement.

During the early 1970s, however, the treasure trove

TRAVELING COMPANION

Curtis and his daughter Beth Curtis Magnuson sailed north from Nome, Alaska, on the Jewel Guard in 1927.

Edward Curtis was often away from his family, but he had a good relationship with his children. He was perhaps closest to his daughter Beth. She had started working in her father's studio as a teenager, and then ran it for several years. Later, with her husband Manford Magnuson, Beth managed the studio that Curtis founded after he moved to Los Angeles. Eventually she and Manford ran three studios with the Curtis name.

While her parents were divorcing, Beth took the drastic step of making prints from some of her father's glass negatives, then destroying the negatives. Curtis biographers believed Beth did not want her mother to make any money selling prints from those negatives.

Beth accompanied her father on his 1927 trip to Alaska. While on the trip, she wrote: "And so it really seems that at last I am about to realize a life long ambition. A trip into Indian country with Dad—only more than I expected for it is to be on a boat."

of Curtis material came to light. Karl Kernberger, an art collector in Santa Fe, New Mexico, heard about the Curtis negatives and prints in Boston. He and a group of investors bought the set and put some items on display. Around this time the country as a whole had regained interest in Indian art and culture. Indians themselves had asserted their political rights during the 1960s, with the founding of the American Indian Movement. The organization wanted the U.S. government to respect the treaties it had made with tribes decades before and to give back tribal lands that had been illegally taken. An older organization, the National Congress of American Indians, had already worked to persuade the U.S. government to pay more attention to Indian concerns.

The public display of Curtis' work in Santa Fe and, even earlier, at the Morgan Library in New York brought new attention to the artistry of the Shadow Catcher. In the summer of 1972, *The New York Times* noted that several new books were being published about Curtis and *The North American Indian*. Two years later a documentary about "the Cause" appeared. Along with showing Curtis' work, the film included interviews with three Indians who had appeared in Curtis' film of the Kwakiutl. More exhibits appeared, with critics praising Curtis' skill. Interest in his photography and grueling adventures to complete *The North American Indian* continued to grow.

But not everyone applauded Curtis and how he had depicted Indian life. In his 1982 book *The Vanishing Race and Other Illusions,* Christopher Lyman said Curtis' work was flawed ethnography. By focusing on pictorialist style and artistic concerns, Lyman thought, Curtis sometimes distorted reality. Curtis changed it by cropping some pictures—cutting out of the frame some of the elements that surrounded his main subject. In some cases Curtis retouched photos to remove items of modern life that had gotten into the picture frame. In a famous example, before he made a print for his book, Curtis removed a clock that sat between two Piegans inside their tent.

Sometimes Curtis made Indians wear clothing or hold props that were not part of their daily lives. In one case, the same headdress appeared on members of two tribes. Critics said Curtis was not trying to show Indians as they really were when he photographed them. They believed he was trying to make the Indians fit his and other whites' ideas of what Indians had been. Even the idea of a "vanishing race" was not accurate. The number of Indians in the country reached its low point in 1900, but has been rising ever since. Census estimates from 2012 show that there are about 2.5 million American Indians and Alaska natives in the U.S. population. More than twice that many people have some native ancestry, bringing the total to 5.2 million.

American Indians weren't vanishing in Curtis' day, but certainly their lives were changing. Curtis rarely photographed them as they adapted to that change. He often criticized the treatment the Indians received

A photo of Little Plume and his son Yellow Kidney changed before it appeared in *The North American Indian*. The alarm clock in the original picture (right) was replaced by a basket when it was published in Volume 6.

from the government and missionaries. But to critics like Lyman and others, he held racist ideas about Native Americans because he would not accept them for who they were.

Some critics also blasted the idea that a true ethnologist would pay to photograph subjects or pose them exactly as he wanted. James C. Faris, in his 1996 book, *Navajo and Photography: A Critical History of the Representation of an American People*, noted that Curtis had some Navajo dances staged for him—they were not performed when they traditionally would have been. Summing up some of the criticism of Curtis, Gerald Vizenor, a professor of American studies at the University of California, wrote in 2000, "Curtis was clearly a photographic faker by his removal and insertions of details, and by false captions."

While Curtis knowingly changed some of what he saw, in at least one instance he was fooled by his subjects. In 1904 he shot film of some Navajo performing the Yeibechei healing dance—the first time it had been captured on film. Almost a century later, a Navajo medicine man explained that the dancers had done the steps backward. Most likely they did not want Curtis to depict the actual ceremony.

While some scholars and American Indians found fault with Curtis' work, many tribes were grateful for *The North American Indian*. Some modern Indians display in their homes the images that Curtis took. They like to

A photo and biographical sketch of Horse Capture appeared in Volume 5. The Atsina warrior was born in 1858.

see how their tribal members once lived, even if Curtis did not always show complete reality. The owners of some prints are related to the Indians shown in them. Joseph D. Horse Capture proudly displays a Curtis picture of his great-great-grandfather, Horse Capture. "Seeing his face," Joseph Horse Capture said, "not only reminds us of our relatives but also reinforces our commitment, as Indian people, to teach our children the ways of our ancestors."

Another fan of Curtis is the American Indian author N. Scott Momaday. He recalled that, when looking at a Curtis picture of Plains Indians, as his Kiowa tribe was, tears had come to his eyes. He related to the people in the picture, and he appreciated the beauty of Curtis' art. Momaday said, "Taken as a whole, the work of Edward

Curtis explained in a caption in Volume 18 that a painted tepee was prized by the northern Plains Assiniboine. The figures were seen in a dream and then painted.

Curtis is a singular achievement. Never before have we seen the Indians of North America so close to the origins of their humanity, their sense of themselves in the world, their innate dignity and self-possession."

Across the West tribal offices and other buildings display Curtis pictures. His work has helped some tribes re-create dances and other traditional events they had abandoned. Tribes of the Pacific Northwest began whale hunting again using the old methods. Piegans of Canada began to hold the Sun Dance again. Some Inuit listened to the recordings Curtis made of the old songs and began to sing them again.

Before writing the photographer's life story, Curtis biographer Timothy Egan visited all the tribes that Curtis had. He said the academics were misguided in not seeing the value in Curtis' photographs. "Go to the subjects themselves," he said. "They appreciate the photos."

Art collectors have shown their appreciation too. A single print of Chief Joseph sold for $160,000 in 2010. Two years later a complete set of *The North American Indian* sold for $1.44 million. But the real value of Curtis' work, Egan and others think, goes beyond the beauty of a single photograph, or even the entire collection. Egan said Curtis helped American Indians "because he showed proof that they were multidimensional people, not savages or poor innocent victims. ... His goal was to make Indians live forever, and I think that's exactly what he did."

Timeline

1868

Edward Sheriff Curtis is born February 16 near Whitewater, Wisconsin

1887

Curtis and his father move from Minnesota to Washington state

1891

Curtis buys into and later owns a photo studio in Seattle

1899

On an expedition to Alaska, Curtis takes several thousand photos of the wilderness and the native people there

1900

In Montana, Curtis photographs the Blackfeet Sun Dance and begins to develop the idea for *The North American Indian*

1892

Curtis marries Clara Phillips; they will have four children

1895

Curtis takes his first photo of an American Indian, Princess Angeline

1903

In Seattle, Chief Joseph poses for Curtis

1904

Curtis photographs President Theodore Roosevelt and his family at their Sagamore Hill home and wins Roosevelt's support for *The North American Indian*

Timeline

58

1906

Banker J.P. Morgan agrees to finance Curtis' project

1907

The first volume of *The North American Indian* is published

1927

Curtis returns to Alaska to shoot photos for the last volume of *The North American Indian,* which is published in 1930

1928

Curtis gives legal control over his materials for *The North American Indian* to the Morgan Company

1909

Curtis and his wife separate; they divorce in 1919

1914

Curtis releases *In the Land of the Head Hunters,* the first film to show elements of Indian life in the Pacific Northwest

1920

Curtis moves to Los Angeles and opens a photo studio with his daughter Beth

1935

The Morgan Company sells all the Curtis material it owns to Boston bookseller Charles E. Lauriat Jr.

1952

Curtis dies in Los Angeles on October 19

Glossary

composition—the arrangement of objects and background that fill a photograph

cropping—the act of trimming away part of a photo to exclude some elements or emphasize others

ethnography—the study and recording of human cultures

Great Plains—the broad, level land that stretches eastward from the base of the Rocky Mountains for about 400 miles (644 kilometers) in the United States and Canada

missionaries—people who try to spread their religious beliefs to others

multidimensional—complex; having many layers or dimensions

negative—photographic image; areas that are light in the original subject are dark in a negative and those that are dark are light; prints can be made from negatives

photogravure—a process of making prints that involves etching the photographic image onto copper plates covered with chemicals

pictorialism—style of photography in the late 19th and early 20th centuries that stressed creating pictures that seemed like paintings rather than images of reality

portfolio—a collection of photographs or other pieces of art by one artist

prints—paper versions of photographs that can be handled or framed

shaman—a tribal religious leader and healer

Additional Resources

Further Reading

Biskup, Agnieszka. *Thunder Rolling Down the Mountain: The Story of Chief Joseph and the Nez Perce*. Mankato, Minn.: Capstone Press, 2011.

Edwards, Laurie J., ed. *UXL Encyclopedia of Native American Tribes*. Detroit: UXL, 2012.

Gulbrandsen, Don. *Edward Sheriff Curtis: Visions of the First Americans*. Edison, N.J.: Chartwell Books, 2010.

Robinson, Charles M. *Battle on the Plains: The United States Plains Wars*. New York: Rosen Pub., 2011.

Spilsbury, Richard. *Geronimo*. Chicago: Raintree, 2014.

Internet Sites

Use FactHound to find Internet sites related to this book. All of the sites on FactHound have been researched by our staff.

Here's all you do:
Visit *www.facthound.com*
Type in this code: 9780756549923

Critical Thinking Using the Common Core

What did Edward S. Curtis mean on page 6 when he said, "The spirit of the Apache is not broken"? What had Geronimo and his Apache people suffered, and how had they survived? (Integration of Knowledge and Ideas)

Compare and contrast the Curtis photos on pages 13 and 18. How does *Homeward* on page 13 fit the pictorialism style? How does its style differ from the portrait of Honovi on page 18? (Craft and Structure)

Curtis has been criticized for romanticizing the American Indians he photographed. What does that mean? Does having a romantic view of them make his photographs less important today? Consider your answer in light of the various views some critics have about his work. (Key Ideas and Details)

Source Notes

Page 5, caption: Edward S. Curtis. *The North American Indian.* Vol. 1, portfolio 1, plate no. 2. Northwestern University Digital Library Collections. http://curtis.library.northwestern.edu/curtis/viewPage.cgi?showp=1&size=2&id=nai.01.port.00000003.p&volume=1

Page 6, line 12: Timothy Egan. *Short Nights of the Shadow Catcher: The Epic Life and Immortal Photographs of Edward Curtis.* Boston: Houghton Mifflin Harcourt, 2012, p. 98.

Page 6, line 21: Ibid., p. 55.

Page 7, caption: *The North American Indian.* Vol. 1, portfolio 1, plate no. 9. http://curtis.library.northwestern.edu/curtis/viewPage.cgi?showp=1&size=2&id=nai.01.port.00000010.p&type=port&volume=1

Page 9, line 1: *Short Nights of the Shadow Catcher: The Epic Life and Immortal Photographs of Edward Curtis,* p. 90.

Page 11, line 2: Anne Makepeace. *Edward S. Curtis: Coming to Light.* Washington, D.C.: National Geographic, 2002, p. 29.

Page 13, col. 1, line 10: Ibid., p. 30.

Page 15, line 1: Mick Gidley, ed. *Edward S. Curtis and the North American Indian Project in the Field.* Lincoln: University of Nebraska Press, 2003, p. 59.

Page 15, line 8: *Edward S. Curtis: Coming to Light,* p. 46.

Page 16, caption: *The North American Indian.* Vol. 6, portfolio 6, plate no. 209. http://curtis.library.northwestern.edu/curtis/viewPage.cgi?showp=1&size=2&id=nai.06.port.0000027.p&type=port&volume=6

Page 18, caption: *The North American Indian.* Vol. 12, portfolio 12, plate no. 408. http://curtis.library.northwestern.edu/curtis/viewPage.cgi?showp=1&size=2&id=nai.12.port.00000010.p&type=port&volume=12

Page 21, caption: *The North American Indian.* Vol. 8, portfolio 8, plate no. 256. http://curtis.library.northwestern.edu/curtis/viewPage.cgi?showp=1&size=2&id=nai.08.port.00000002.p&volume=8

Page 21, line 5: *Short Nights of the Shadow Catcher: The Epic Life and Immortal Photographs of Edward Curtis,* p. 69.

Page 22, line 15: *Edward S. Curtis: Coming to Light,* p. 50.

Page 23, line 6: Theodore Roosevelt. *Theodore Roosevelt: An Autobiography.* New York: Charles Scribner's Sons, 1920, p. 93.

Page 25, col. 1, line 8: Edmund Morris. *The Rise of Theodore Roosevelt.* New York: Modern Library, 2001, p. 476.

Page 25, col. 2, line 8: Theodore Roosevelt. *The Rough Riders.* New York: Charles Scribner's Sons, 1899, p. 41.

Page 26, line 6: *The North American Indian.* Vol. 1, p. xi. http://curtis.library.northwestern.edu/curtis/viewPage.cgi?showp=1&size=2&id=nai.01.book.00000015&volume=1

Page 26, line 15: Mick Gidley. *Edward S. Curtis and the North American Indian, Incorporated.* Cambridge: Cambridge University Press, 1998, p. 62.

Page 26, line 23: *Edward S. Curtis: Coming to Light,* p. 56.

Page 29, line 21: *Short Nights of the Shadow Catcher: The Epic Life and Immortal Photographs of Edward Curtis,* p. 114.

Page 31, caption: *The North American Indian.* Vol. 1, portfolio 1, plate no. 1. http://curtis.library.northwestern.edu/curtis/viewPage.cgi?showp=1&size=2&id=nai.01.port.00000002.p&type=port&volume=1

Page 31, line 2: Ibid.

Page 32, caption: *The North American Indian.* Vol. 1, portfolio 1, plate no. 28. http://curtis.library.northwestern.edu/curtis/viewPage.cgi?showp=1&size=2&id=nai.01.port.00000029.p&volume=1#nav

Page 33, line 10: *The North American Indian.* Vol. 1, p. xv. http://curtis.library.northwestern.edu/curtis/viewPage.cgi?showp=1&size=2&id=nai.01.book.00000021&volume=1#nav xiv

Page 33, lines 20 and 23: Ibid.

Page 34, caption: *The North American Indian.* Vol. 1, portfolio 1, plate no. 22. http://curtis.library.northwestern.edu/curtis/viewPage.cgi?showp=1&size=2&id=nai.01.port.00000023.p&type=port&volume=1

Page 35, line 8: "American Indian in 'Photo History'; Mr. Edward Curtis's $3,000 Work on the Aborigine a Marvel of Pictorial Record." *The New York Times.* 6 June 1908. 30 Sept. 2014. http://query.nytimes.com/mem/archive-free/pdf?res=F50D12F73F5A17738DDDAF0894DE405B888CF1D3

Page 35, line13: *Short Nights of the Shadow Catcher: The Epic Life and Immortal Photographs of Edward Curtis,* p. 155.

Page 37, line 2: Edward S. Curtis. "Vanishing Indian Types." *Scribners Magazine.* June 1906, p. 660. 30 Sept. 2014. http://www.unz.org/Pub/Scribners-1906jun-00657?View=Contents

Page 39, line 18: *Edward S. Curtis and the North American Indian Project in the Field,* p. 67.

Page 44, line 22: Ibid., p. 121.

Page 46, line 8: *Short Nights of the Shadow Catcher: The Epic Life and Immortal Photographs of Edward Curtis,* p. 308.

Page 46, line 27: Ibid., p. 308.

Page 47, lines 2 and 6: Special to The New York Times. "Edward S. Curtis." *The New York Times.* 20 Oct. 1952, p. 23.

Page 48, col. 2, line 6: *Edward S. Curtis and the North American Indian Project in the Field.,* p. 116.

Page 52, line 14: Gerald Vizenor. "Edward Curtis: Pictorialist and Ethnographic Adventurist." Edward S. Curtis in Context. Library of Congress. October 2000. 30 Sept. 2014. http://memory.loc.gov/ammem/award98/ienhtml/essay3.html

Page 53, line 5: "Native Americans on Curtis." Edward Curtis Photography, Life and Work. Cardozo Fine Art. 30 Sept. 2014. http://www.edwardcurtis.com/native-americans-on-curtis/

Page 54, line 6: Ibid.

Page 55, line 16: Wolf Schneider. "Edward Curtis Revisited." *Cowboys and Indians Magazine.* April 2013. 30 Sept. 2014. http://www.cowboysindians.com/Cowboys-Indians/April-2013/Edward-Curtis-Revisited/Author-Timothy-Egan-discusses-his-biography/

Page 55, line 24: Ibid.

Select Bibliography

"American Indian Tribal List: Native American Indian Tribes and Languages." Native Languages of the Americas. http://www.native-languages.org/languages.htm

Brust, James S., Brian C. Pohanka, and Sandy Barnard. *Where Custer Fell: Photographs of the Little Bighorn Battlefield Then and Now*. Norman: University of Oklahoma Press, 2005.

Coleman, A. D. "From Indians to Activists." *The New York Times*, 16 July 1972, p. D12.

Curtis, Edward S. *The North American Indian*. Los Angeles: Taschen, 2005.

Curtis, Edward S. *The North American Indian*. 20 volumes. Northwestern University Digital Library Collections. http://curtis.library.northwestern.edu/

Daniels, Valerie. "Selling the North American Indian: The Work of Edward S. Curtis." American Studies at the University of Virginia. June 2002. 30 Sept. 2014. http://xroads.virginia.edu/~ma02/daniels/curtis/introduction.html

"Edward S. Curtis's The North American Indian." American Memory. Library of Congress. http://memory.loc.gov/ammem/award98/ienhtml/curthome.html

Egan, Timothy. *Short Nights of the Shadow Catcher: The Epic Life and Immortal Photographs of Edward Curtis*. Boston: Houghton Mifflin Harcourt, 2012.

Faris, James C. *Navajo and Photography: A Critical History of the Representation of an American People*. Albuquerque: University of New Mexico Press, 1996.

"Frontier Photographer: Edward S. Curtis." Smithsonian Institution Libraries. http://www.sil.si.edu/Exhibitions/Curtis/index.htm

Gidley, Mick. *Edward S. Curtis and the North American Indian, Incorporated*. Cambridge: Cambridge University Press, 1998.

Gidley, Mick, ed. *Edward S. Curtis and the North American Indian Project in the Field*. Lincoln: University of Nebraska Press, 2003.

Grundberg, Andy. "More Than Meets the Eye." *The New York Times*. 5 Sept. 1982. 30 Sept. 2014. http://www.nytimes.com/1982/09/05/books/more-than-meets-the-eye.html

Hirschfelder, Arlene, and Paulette Molin. *Encyclopedia of Native American Religions*. New York: Facts on File, 2000.

Josephy, Alvin M., Jr. *500 Nations: An Illustrated History of North American Indians*. New York: Knopf, 1994.

Lyman, Christopher M. *The Vanishing Race and Other Illusions: Photographs of Indians by Edward S. Curtis*. Washington, D.C.: Smithsonian Institution Press, 1982.

Makepeace, Anne. *Edward S. Curtis: Coming to Light*. Washington, D.C.: National Geographic, 2002.

Morris, Edmund. *The Rise of Theodore Roosevelt*. New York: Modern Library, 2001.

"Pictorialism." The Art of Photography. http://theartofphotography.tv/episodes/pictorialism/

"Pictorialism in America." Heilbrunn Timeline of American History. The Metropolitan Museum of Art. http://www.metmuseum.org/toah/hd/pict/hd_pict.htm#slideshow6

Schneider, Wolf. "Edward Curtis Revisited." *Cowboys and Indians Magazine*. April 2013. 30 Sept. 2014. http://www.cowboysindians.com/Cowboys-Indians/April-2013/Edward-Curtis-Revisited/Author-Timothy-Egan-discusses-his-biography/

Zamir, Shamoon. "Native Agency and the Making of 'The North American Indian': Alexander B. Upshaw and Edward S. Curtis." *American Indian Quarterly*. Vol. 31, No. 4. Fall 2007, pp. 613–653.

Index

About the Author

Michael Burgan has written many books for children and young adults during his 20 years as a freelance writer. Many of his books have focused on history. Michael has won several awards for his writing. He lives in Santa Fe, New Mexico.